RON WHEELER

BEACON HILL PRESS OF KANSAS CITY
KANSAS CITY, MISSOURI

THE ADVENTURES OF...

JEREMIAH

by ©1988
Wheeler
H-6

LUKE WAKES UP WITH A KNOT IN HIS STOMACH.

OH NO! IT'S MORNING ALREADY!

MAYBE I'M STILL DREAMING AND IT'S STILL THE MIDDLE OF THE NIGHT.

NOPE. IT'S MORNING ALL RIGHT.

RRIINGG!

OH, I DREAD GETTING OUT OF BED TODAY.

MAYBE THIS ISN'T THE RIGHT DAY.

MAYBE IT'S NEXT WEEK.

NOPE! I WAS RIGHT. TODAY IS THE DAY.

THE ADVENTURES OF...

JEREMIAH

by ©1988 Wheeler
H-7

FOR THEIR MID-TERM EXAM STUDENTS HAVE TO GIVE A SPEECH BEFORE THE **WHOLE** CLASS, AND LUKE HAS STAGE FRIGHT.

AS YOU KNOW...

OH, DREAD! DREAD! DREAD!

...TODAY'S SPEECHES...

I WOULD RATHER BE ANYWHERE THAN HERE RIGHT NOW.

...WILL BE GIVEN BEFORE THE WHOLE CLASS...

I HATE GIVING SPEECHES.

...AND WILL CONSTITUTE A MAJOR PORTION OF YOUR GRADE.

NOW HOLD ON, LUKE THAT'S NOT A CHRISTIAN ATTITUDE.

POINTS WILL BE GIVEN ON STYLE, CONTENT, AND DELIVERY.

EVEN THOUGH YOU AREN'T VERY GOOD AT THIS, YOU CAN HANDLE IT.

SO, JUST RELAX...

JUST RELAX! SEE?

THE ADVENTURES OF...

JEREMIAH
©1988
by
Ray Wheeler
H-8

LUKE IS CALLED UPON TO GIVE HIS SPEECH BEFORE THE **WHOLE** CLASS.

LUKE, WOULD YOU GIVE US YOUR SPEECH?

I KNEW IT! I KNEW SHE'D PICK ME FIRST!

THE LONGEST TIME IN THE WORLD...

...IS THE AMOUNT OF TIME IT TAKES TO WALK...

...FROM YOUR DESK TO THE FRONT OF THE ROOM...

...WHEN YOU KNOW YOU AREN'T PREPARED WELL ENOUGH.

GO AHEAD, LUKE.

GACK!

LUKE?

TO BE CONTINUED...

THE ADVENTURES OF...

JEREMIAH

by ©1988
Ry Wheeler
H-9

LUKE CHOKES WHILE TRYING TO DELIVER HIS TALK IN SPEECH CLASS.

HA! HA! HA! HA!
HA! HA! HA!
HA! HA!
HA!

OKAY, SIT DOWN, LUKE, AND WE'LL LET YOU TRY IT AGAIN LATER.

HOW HUMILIATING!

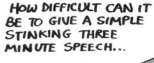

HOW DIFFICULT CAN IT BE TO GIVE A SIMPLE STINKING THREE MINUTE SPEECH...

...BEFORE THIS BUNCH OF YO-YO'S.

BUT NO, LUKE, YOU HAVE TO GET UP AND MAKE A TOTAL IDIOT OF YOURSELF...

LORD, WHY DOES LIFE HAVE TO BE SO HARD?

HELP ME TO HANDLE THIS.

I'M SO DISTRAUGHT I'M NOT EVEN PAYING ATTENTION TO THE OTHER SPEECHES.

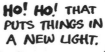

THE ADVENTURES OF... JEREMIAH

by ©1988 RoWheder 4-20

MATT AND LUKE PLAN TO CHEAT ON THE BIG TEST BY HIDING ANSWERS IN THE TOWEL RACK IN THE BATHROOM.

WINK WINK

...HOWEVER, THEIR PLANS TURN AWRY WHEN JEREMIAH'S BALL POINT PEN BREAKS.

AW NUTS!

MR. THORNBUSH, MAY I BE EXCUSED TO GO TO THE RESTROOM?

SURE, JEREMIAH.

OH NO!

OH NO!

WHAT'S THIS? ...SOME PAPER TOWELS WITH WRITING ON THEM?

OH, WELL, AS LONG AS THEY SERVE THEIR PURPOSE.

WAD WAD SHRED SHRED

MR. THORNBUSH! MR. THORNBUSH!

WHAT IS IT, MATT?

THE ADVENTURES OF...

JEREMIAH

by ©1988 Ron Wheeler 4-21

JEREMIAH GETS A CALL FROM HIS WORLD GOVERNMENT TEACHER.

Y-Y-YOU WANTED TO SEE ME, MR. THORNBUSH?

SIT DOWN, JEREMIAH. I GOT THIS LETTER YESTERDAY.

DEAR MR. THORNBUSH, THIS IS AN ANONYMOUS TIP TO LET YOU KNOW THAT SOMEONE CHEATED ON YOUR LAST EXAM. HINT; HE SPILLED BLUE INK ON HIS HANDS AND GOT A 92%.

WELL, THIS SOUNDS LIKE ME!

I DIDN'T CHEAT, MR. THORNBUSH.

I KNOW YOU DIDN'T, JEREMIAH.

WHO WOULD WRITE SUCH A THING?

APPARENTLY SOMEONE WHO THOUGHT YOU STOLE THEIR ANSWERS OUT OF THE PAPER TOWEL RACK IN THE BATHROOM

PAPER TOWEL RACK?

 THE ADVENTURES OF...

 JEREMIAH

by ©1988
Ron Wheeler
4-22

JEREMIAH IS CRUSHED BECAUSE MATT TRIED TO CHEAT AND THEN ACCUSED JEREMIAH OF IT.

GRAMPS, WHY WOULD MATT DO SOMETHING LIKE THAT?

I DON'T KNOW, JEREMIAH, MATT'S A TOUGH KID TO FIGURE OUT SOMETIMES.

HE'S ALWAYS TRYING TO GET AWAY WITH SOMETHING.

HE LOOKS FOR THE EASY WAY OUT AND IF THAT DOESN'T WORK, THEN HE STARTS TRYING TO MANIPULATE THINGS TO GO HIS WAY.

THEN, AS USUAL, EVERYTHING FALLS APART, BUT HE STILL DOESN'T SEEM TO LEARN.

WHAT CAN I DO TO GET THROUGH TO HIM AND STRAIGHTEN HIM OUT?

PROBABLY NOTHING.

NOTHING? YEAH, I'VE FOUND IN DISCIPLING OTHERS, THERE IS VERY LITTLE I CAN DO OR SAY THAT MAKES ANY LASTING CHANGES IN ANYONE'S LIFE.

MOST OF THE CHANGES I'VE SEEN IN PEOPLE HAVE COME THROUGH PRAYING FOR THEM, GETTING THE WORD OF GOD INTO THEM, AND BY BEING A GOOD EXAMPLE.

THE ADVENTURES OF...

JEREMIAH

by ©1988 Roy Keeler
H-23

LUKE HAS SOME PROFOUND QUESTIONS FOR JEREMIAH.

WHY DID GOD CREATE MOSQUITOES?

WELL, ...UH..

I MEAN...ALL THEY DO IS BITE YOU AND CARRY TROPICAL DISEASES.

THERE ARE PLENTY OF OTHER BUGS BIRDS CAN EAT, WHY DID HE HAVE TO CREATE **THIS** PEST?

WELL...

ALSO, WHY ISN'T CHOCOLATE GOOD FOR YOU AND BROCCOLI THAT GIVES YOU ZITS?

AND... WHY AM I **ALWAYS** TEMPTED TO DO **BAD** THINGS?

WHY DOESN'T TEMPTATION EXIST FOR DOING GOOD THINGS LIKE EATING RIGHT OR STUDYING HARD?

UH...

THE ADVENTURES OF...

JEREMIAH

by © 1988 Wheeler
A-37

PENNY AND TRUDY ENJOY THE FIRST DAY OF SCHOOL.

WHAT DO YOU MEAN?

THE FIRST DAY OF SCHOOL CAN BE QUITE ENTERTAINING TO THOSE WITH A KEEN SENSE OF OBSERVATION.

I LOVE TO WATCH PEOPLE AS THEY COME INTO A NEW CLASSROOM.

SO?

EVERYONE'S GOT THEIR OWN STYLE.

SOME PEOPLE SLITHER INTO THE NEAREST SEAT AND THE GRADUALLY PEEK AROUND THE ROOM TO SEE WHO'S THERE.

ZIP

OTHER PEOPLE LIKE TO COME IN WITH A SPLASH SHOWING OFF THEIR NEW FANCY DUDS AND BEING VERY LOUD SO EVERYONE NOTICES.

HEY, I'M HERE!

ALL OF WHICH IS DONE TO COVER UP MANY DEEP INSECURITIES.

OF COURSE.

THEN THERE ARE THOSE WHO MAKE A BEE-LINE TO THE BACK OF THE ROOM WHERE THEY CAN HIDE.

THEN THERE'S THE AMBITIOUS (OR PERHAPS NEARSIGHTED) TYPES WHO LIKE TO SIT IN FRONT AND ASK QUESTIONS.

I ALSO GET A KICK OUT OF THE EARLY ARRIVALS WHO SIT IN THE MIDDLE AND TRY TO CONTROL WHO SITS OR DOESN'T SIT NEXT TO THEM BY THE EXPRESSION ON THEIR FACE.

THE MOST INTERESTING TO ME ARE THOSE WHO COME IN AT A SLOW EVEN GAIT IN ORDER TO MAKE A QUICK SCAN TO CHECK OUT WHO'S HERE AND WHO'S NOT...

...THOUGH NOT LOOKING AT ANY ONE PERSON FOR TOO LONG LEST THAT INDIVIDUAL THINKS HE/SHE WANTS TO SIT NEXT HIM/HER...

...BUT CAREFULLY, SUBTLEY, AND NONCHALANTLY PICKS JUST THE RIGHT SEAT AFTER MAKING A QUICK ASSESSMENT OF THE PROS AND CONS OF WHO'S IN THE SURROUNDING AREA...

UH-OH NERD AT 3 O'CLOCK.

...WHICH USUALLY JUST HAPPENS TO BE NEXT TO SOMEONE INTERESTING OF THE OPPOSITE GENDER.

I'LL TAKE THIS ONE

BUT WHAT MAKES THIS ALL SO ENTERTAINING IS IT'S ALL WASTED ENERGY...

BECAUSE THIS TEACHER MAKES US ALL SIT IN ALPHABETICAL ORDER ANYWAY.

AWWW (W

A's IN FRONT... LET'S GO PEOPLE!

THE ADVENTURES OF... JEREMIAH

by ©1988 Ron Wheeler 4-39

JEREMIAH TRIES TO CONCENTRATE IN STUDY HALL.

TAP TAP TAP

TAPPITY TAP TAP YEAH

BOOMBA BOOM BAH

MATT, WILL YOU KNOCK IT OFF.

KNOCK WHAT OFF?

YOU'RE MAKING A RACKET AND I'M TRYING TO STUDY.

WELL, EXCUSE ME.

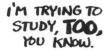

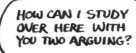

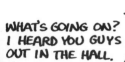

THE ADVENTURES OF...

JEREMIAH

by ©1989
P. Wheeler
I-5

JEREMIAH AND MATT ARE IN ART CLASS.

WHAT'S WRONG, LUKE?

AAAUGH!

I CAN'T GET THIS RIGHT!

WHENEVER I TRY TO PUT ON ONE COLOR IT SMEARS THE ONE I JUST PUT DOWN.

PLUS MY PROPORTIONS AREN'T RIGHT AND THE WHOLE THING LOOKS LIKE SOMEONE SNEEZED ALL OVER IT.

WHAT AM I DOING IN THIS CLASS? I DON'T HAVE ANY TALENT! I'M NO GOOD! I CAN'T DO ANYTHING!

I THINK IT LOOKS FINE.

OH YEAH! YOU'RE JUST SAYING THAT TO MAKE ME FEEL BETTER!

THE ADVENTURES OF...

JEREMIAH

by Jay Wheeler ©1989
I-6

MATT AND JEREMIAH LOOK AT LUKE'S PAINTING.

HERE IT IS! IT'S IN THE PILE THE TEACHER HASN'T GRADED YET.

WELL I DON'T THINK IT LOOKS SO BAD.

IT'S NOT... BUT LUKE HAS A HARD TIME THINKING IT'S ANY GOOD.

WHY? IT'S JUST AN ELEPHANT.

WELL, NO... IT'S A DUCK. IT JUST LOOKS LIKE AN ELEPHANT.

I GUESS HE FEELS SOMEWHAT VULNERABLE BECAUSE HE PUT SO MUCH OF HIS HEART INTO IT.

THAT'S A DUCK?

BUT THAT'S WHAT IT TAKES TO BE GOOD, RIGHT?

EXACTLY! GRAMPS SAYS, "WHATEVER YOU DO, IF YOU WANT IT TO REFLECT YOUR HEART, YOU'VE GOT TO PUT YOUR HEART INTO IT.

YEAH, LUKE'S GOT A PRETTY HEARTFELT DUCK HERE.

I'VE GOT TO GET TO CLASS. SEE YOU LATER, MATT.

RRRRINGG

THE ADVENTURES OF...

JEREMIAH

by ©1989
Kay Wheeler
I-7

LUKE COMES TO JEREMIAH WITH SOME GOOD NEWS.

JEREMIAH, GUESS WHAT?

WHAT?

I GOT AN "A" ON MY PAINTING IN ART CLASS!

GREAT!

PLUS, THEY'RE PUTTING IT ON DISPLAY IN THE CAFETERIA AND PLAN TO ENTER IT IN A REGIONAL ART SHOW THIS SPRING!

WOW! THAT'S FANTASTIC!

THEY'RE UNVEILING IT RIGHT NOW! COME ON!

AND NOW I'D LIKE TO PRESENT TO YOU BENTON HIGH'S REPRESENTATION IN THE REGIONAL ART EXHIBIT THIS SPRING.

IT'S CALLED "AN ABSTRACT DUCK" BY LUKE MULLIGAN.

I CAN'T WATCH, JEREMIAH. I'M TOO EMBARRASSED!

OOO! WOW!

COOL!

THE ADVENTURES OF...

by ©1989
Wheeler
I-8

LUKE MEETS UP WITH MATT.

UH-OH! HERE COMES LUKE! I WONDER IF HE'S SEEN WHAT HAPPENED TO HIS PAINTING.

GACK! I GUESS SO!

I WANNA TALK TO YOU!

LUKE... I'M SORRY I RUINED... I MEAN IT WAS AN... THE WATER WAS ALL OVER... HOW CAN I...

COOL IT! WHAT I WANT TO KNOW IS CAN YOU DO THE SAME THING TO THESE PAINTINGS?

HUH?

YOU WANT ME TO RUIN THESE PAINTINGS TOO?

SURE! IT'S A CLASS ASSIGNMENT.

AFTER YOU SPLASHED WATER AND PAINT ON MY OTHER PAINTING, I THOUGHT OF TAKING CREDIT MYSELF FOR IMPROVING IT...

THE ADVENTURES OF...

JEREMIAH

by
MWheeler
I-21

JEREMIAH IS OVER AT LUKE'S HOUSE.

ARE YOU READY TO GO, LUKE?

YEAH... LET ME SEE NOW...

OH, I ALMOST FORGOT!

WAIT A SECOND, JEREMIAH. THERE'S SOMETHING I NEED TO DO FIRST.

FLIP FLIP

SCRIBBLE SCRIBBLE

OKAY, NOW I'M READY.

WHAT WAS THAT ALL ABOUT?

TO BE CONTINUED...

THE ADVENTURES OF... JEREMIAH

by ©1989 Tony Wheeler I-22

LUKE IS FULL OF WORRY.

OH WORRY! WORRY! WORRY!

I'LL NEVER GET THIS TERM PAPER DONE ON TIME!

I'VE GOT TO TAKE A BREAK.

MAYBE IF I CLOSE MY EYES FOR JUST A FEW MINUTES...

AND LUKE BEGINS TO DREAM

ZZZ ZZZZ

YIKES! LOOK AT THE TIME! I'VE GOT TO GET BACK TO WORK!

I CAN'T WORK YET.

I NEED SOME FRESH AIR!

YES, THAT'S IT...FRESH AIR.

TO BE CONTINUED...

THE ADVENTURES OF...

JEREMIAH

by ©1989
Wheeler
1-23

LUKE IS DREAMING.

LOUIE SAID I COULD GET A TERM PAPER HERE.

WELL HERE GOES.

YEAH?

UH... LOUIE SENT ME.

WHATTYA WANT?

H-HE SAID I COULD GET A TERM PAPER HERE BUT...

WHAT'S THE SUBJECT?

YOU SEE, THAT'S JUST IT. I'M SURE YOU DON'T...

WHAT'S THE SUBJECT?

"THE EFFECTS OF WATER FLUORIDATION ON HAMPSTER TEETH"!

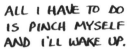

THE ADVENTURES OF...

JEREMIAH

by ©1990
Ron Wheeler
I-34

JEREMIAH IS THE VICTIM OF AN EXTORTIONIST.

GACK!

HEY, SHRIMP, GIMME A DOLLAR AND I'LL LET YOU LIVE!

HEY, WHY DON'T YOU PICK ON SOMEONE YOUR OWN SIZE?

OKAY, I'LL PICK ON YOU!

NOT ME! I'M NOT YOUR SIZE.

OKAY, I'LL PICK ON BOTH OF YOU, YOU CAN EACH GIVE ME A BUCK.

OOPS! THERE'S THE BELL.

SORRY, WE HAVE TO GO.

RRRIIINNGGG

YOU'RE LUCKY THIS TIME. I'LL SEE YOU TWO AFTER SCHOOL.

TO BE CONTINUED...

THE ADVENTURES OF...

JEREMIAH

by ©1990
Tom Wheeler
I-35

MATT IS AFRAID OF GETTING MUGGED AFTER SCHOOL BY A BULLY NAMED BIFF.

MATT, WHAT ARE YOU DOING?

I'M JUST KEEPING AN EYE OUT FOR THAT BULLY WHO TRIED TO GET MONEY FROM US THIS MORNING.

I THOUGHT I TOLD YOU NOT TO WORRY ABOUT HIM.

THAT'S EASY FOR YOU TO SAY. YOU'RE NOT WALKING AROUND WITH A BIG WAD OF DOUGH.

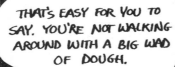

HEY, WHERE DID YOU GET THAT?

MATT, HAVE YOU BEEN GAMBLING AGAIN?

NO! NO! NO!

THIS IS MONEY MY GRANDMA GAVE ME TO PAY HER RENT ON THE WAY HOME FROM SCHOOL TODAY.

IT'S ALL SHE HAS UNTIL HER NEXT PENSION CHECK.

SHE FORGOT TO MAIL IN HER RENT CHECK LAST MONTH...

...AND IF SOMEONE DOESN'T PAY IT BY 5:00 PM TODAY, SHE GETS THROWN OUT OF HER APARTMENT.

WOW!

NOW I KNOW WHY YOU'VE BEEN SO NERVOUS ABOUT THAT BULLY TODAY.

EXACTLY!

IF ANYTHING HAPPENS TO THIS MONEY...

...I'M IN HOT SOUP!

I HOPE YOU BROUGHT CRACKERS.

TO BE CONTINUED...

THE ADVENTURES OF...

JEREMIAH

by ©1990
Tom Wheeler
I-36

MATT, WITH A BIG WAD OF MONEY, FINDS HIMSELF IN HOT SOUP.

DON'T LOOK NOW, MATT...

EEEEEK!

HEY, SQUIRT, WHERE YA BEEN HIDIN'? I'VE BEEN LOOKIN' FOR YOU.

HIDING? ME HIDING? I WASN'T HIDING!

WHAT'S THAT YOU GOT IN YOUR HAND?

HAND? WHAT HAND? I DON'T HAVE ANY HAND!

WHERE'S THAT DOLLAR YOU PROMISED ME?

DOLLAR? DID I PROMISE YOU A PROMISE?

YEAH, SORT OF PROTECTION INSURANCE, YA KNOW?

PROTECTION INSURANCE?

TO BE CONTINUED...

THE ADVENTURES OF...

JEREMIAH

by © 1990 Ron Wheeler

I-37

BIFF FINDS OUT MATT HAS A WAD OF MONEY ON HIM.

HEY YOU! COME BACK HERE!

OH NO! IT'S BIFF!

YOU'RE HOLDIN' OUT ON ME!

LET'S MAKE A RUN FOR IT, JEREMIAH.

YOU CAN RUN BUT YOU CAN'T HIDE!

I'LL JUST GET YOU TOMORROW, RICH KID.

WHAT AM I GOING TO DO, JEREMIAH?

HE THINKS I CARRY MONEY AROUND LIKE THIS ALL THE TIME.

YEAH HE DOESN'T SEEM THE TYPE TO BELIEVE THAT WAD IS YOUR GRANDMA'S RENT MONEY.

PANT PANT

..OR SHOULD YOU WANT TO LOVE HIM SO HE CAN BECOME A CHRISTIAN?

WHOA! I GUESS YOU'RE RIGHT.

BUT HOW DO YOU LOVE A GUY LIKE THAT?

WELL THE MAIN THING HE NEEDS IS TOUGH LOVE.

YOU HAVE TO STAND UP TO HIM AND NOT LET HIM PUSH YOU AROUND ANYMORE.

BEING A CHRISTIAN DOESN'T MEAN YOU'RE A DOORMAT FOR EVERY BULLY.

YOU'RE RIGHT, JEREMIAH, I'M GOING TO STAND UP TO HIM...

...FIRST THING TOMORROW.

GIVE ME A BUCK, RICH KID, OR I'LL RIP YOUR THUMBS OFF.

TO BE CONTINUED...

THE ADVENTURES OF...

JEREMIAH

by ©1990
Wheeler
I-39

MATT FINALLY STANDS UP TO THE BULLY.

GIVE ME A DOLLAR RICH KID OR I'LL REARRANGE YOUR FACE.

NO!

WHAT DID YOU SAY?

GACK! NO!

WHAT DO YOU MEAN, "NO!" THAT'S NOT HOW WE DO BUSINESS HERE!

WELL, WE'RE NO LONGER DOING BUSINESS, BIFF.

YOU CAN TRY TO BEAT ME UP IF YOU LIKE BUT I'M NOT GOING TO BE AFRAID OF YOU ANYMORE.

BOY, YOU'RE WRITING YOUR DEATH CERTIFICATE, BUDDY.

THAT MAY BE TRUE, BUT I'D RATHER DIE FOR A GOOD CAUSE, THEN LIVE FOR A BAD ONE.

THE ADVENTURES OF...
JEREMIAH

by ©1990
Roy Wheeler
J-3

MATT DECIDES NOT TO WALK HOME FROM SCHOOL WITH JEREMIAH TODAY.

SORRY, JEREMIAH, TREVOR HALEY IS GIVING ME A RIDE.

TREVOR HALEY?

ISN'T HE THE GUY WHO WAS SUSPENDED FOR THREE DAYS FOR FIGHTING?

YEAH, BUT IT WASN'T HIS FAULT. HE REALLY IS A NICE GUY.

SURE! SURE!

SEE YA LATER, JEREMIAH

HEY, TREVOR, IT SURE IS NICE OF YOU TO GIVE ME A RIDE.

GET IN.

HI, GUYS, HOW'S IT GOIN'

GRUNT

THE ADVENTURES OF...

JEREMIAH

by © 1990
Roy Wheeler
J-4

MATT'S NEW "FRIENDS" TAKE A DETOUR ON THEIR WAY HOME FROM SCHOOL.

SMASH

WHAT ARE YOU... CRAZY?

YOU GUYS DELIBERATELY BROKE MR. THORNBUSH'S CAR WINDOWS!

HA! HA!

HA! HA!

HEE! HEE! HEE!

TAKE ME HOME NOW!

HA HA

HA HA

COME ON, LIGHTEN UP, MATT. THIS IS FUN!

YEAH, SOME FUN.

HERE! YOU WANNA THROW ONE?

NO WAY!

OKAY, I'LL DO IT.

WAIT!

TO BE CONTINUED...

THE ADVENTURES OF...
JEREMIAH

by ©1990 Wheeler
J-5

JEREMIAH APPROACHES MATT WITH SOME NEWS.

MATT, DID YOU HEAR? SOMEONE THREW BRICKS THRU MR. THORNBUSH'S WINDSHIELD.

OH REALLY?

WELL, YOU DON'T SEEM VERY SURPRISED.

ME? NO...UH... REALLY! THAT'S REALLY SOMETHING!

SOMEONE BROKE OUT THE WINDSHIELD, HUH? WOW! WHO WOULD DO THAT?

SAY...

YOU KNOW SOMETHING ABOUT THIS, DON'T YOU?

ME? HOW WOULD I KNOW ANYTHING ABOUT SOMETHING LIKE THAT?

BECAUSE YOU'RE ACTING AWFULLY STRANGE.

STRANGE? ME? STRANGE?

I'LL BET YOU KNOW WHO DID IT!

TO BE CONTINUED...

THE ADVENTURES OF... JEREMIAH

by ©1990
Ron Wheeler
J-6

MATT IS CONFRONTED BY TREVOR HALEY.

HEY, MATT!

EEEEK!

I HEAR AN UGLY RUMOR FLOATING AROUND SCHOOL THAT I BROKE MR. THORN-BUSH'S WINDSHIELD.

GULP!

NOW WHERE DO YOU SUPPOSE PEOPLE WOULD GET AN IDEA LIKE THAT?

I DIDN'T SAY ANYTHING!

ESPECIALLY WHEN THE ONLY PERSON WHO COULD HAVE POSSIBLY SAID ANYTHING WOULD BE YOU?

I DIDN'T TELL ANYBODY YOU BROKE THE WINDSHIELD.

OF COURSE YOU DIDN'T BECAUSE THAT WOULD BE A LIE.

REMEMBER, WE TALKED ABOUT THIS, MATT. THE BOYS AND I AGREED YOU WERE THE ONE WHO THREW THE BRICKS, WEREN'T YOU?

YEAH, WHAT'S HE... SAY!

JESUS WAS INNOCENT AND HE SUFFERED UNJUSTLY, DIDN'T HE?

YES, AND LOOK AT WHAT PAUL SAID.

"I WANT TO KNOW CHRIST AND THE POWER OF HIS RESURRECTION AND THE FELLOWSHIP OF SHARING IN HIS DEATH, AND SO, SOMEHOW, TO ATTAIN THE RESURRECTION FROM THE DEAD." *

* PHIL. 3:10, 11

WOW! YOU MEAN SOMEHOW BY SUFFERING UNJUSTLY I CAN IDENTIFY MORE WITH CHRIST AND KNOW HIM BETTER?

EXACTLY!

OH BOY!

WHAT ARE YOU EXCITED ABOUT?

I JUST REALIZED I HAVEN'T TOLD MY PARENTS I'VE BEEN SUSPENDED FROM SCHOOL YET.

NOW, I'LL BE ABLE TO EXPERIENCE SOME REAL UNJUST SUFFERING.

HE'S NUTS, YOU KNOW.

TO BE CONTINUED...

THE ADVENTURES OF...

JEREMIAH

by ©1990
DWheeler
J-8

MR. THORNBUSH VISITS WITH MATT.

MATT, DO YOU KNOW WHY I SUSPENDED YOU?

BECAUSE YOU THINK I SMASHED YOUR WINDSHIELD.

NO, I KNOW TREVOR HALEY SMASHED MY CAR WINDOWS.

YOU DO?

WELL THEN, WHY DON'T YOU PUNISH HIM?

HE'S ALREADY BEING DISCIPLINED. HE'S IN REFORM SCHOOL NOW.

REFORM SCHOOL?

TREVOR GOT INTO LOTS OF FIGHTS AND HAS HAD PLENTY OF CHANCES TO STRAIGHTEN OUT.

HIS PARENTS AND I FELT THAT REFORM SCHOOL WAS BETTER EQUIPPED TO DEAL WITH HIS PROBLEMS.

THE ADVENTURES OF...

JEREMIAH

by ©1990 Roy Wheeler J-18

MR. THORNBUSH ANNOUNCES HE WILL BE GONE FOR A FEW DAYS.

I HAVE A SPECIAL SEMINAR OUT OF TOWN BUT I CAN ASSURE YOU...

...MISS HAZELWOOD WILL HAVE MATTERS WELL IN HAND WHILE I'M GONE.

DID YOU HEAR THAT, LUKE?

WE'RE GOING TO GET A SUB!

SO?

WHILE THE CAT'S AWAY THE MICE WILL PLAY.

BUT WE'RE SCHEDULED TO HAVE A TEST WHILE HE'S GONE.

NOT WHEN WE GET THROUGH WITH OLD MISS HAZELNUT.

I BELIEVE IT'S HAZELWOOD

I CAN SEE HER NOW. SHE'S PROBABLY SOME NINETY YEAR OLD LADY WITH COKE BOTTLE GLASSES AND ORTHOPEDIC SHOES.

THE ADVENTURES OF...

JEREMIAH

by ©1990
Ron Wheeler
J-19

LUKE AND MATT CONSPIRE TO GIVE THE NEW SUBSTITUTE TEACHER A HARD TIME.

THIS IS GREAT! THIS IS GREAT!

THESE FAKE SPIDERS WILL SCARE THE GERITAL OUT OF THE OLD LADY.

AND THIS RUBBER SNAKE WILL SHOCK THE OIL OF OLAY RIGHT OUT OF HER WRINKLES.

AND OF COURSE THE FAKE VOMIT WILL STARTLE THE FALSE TEETH RIGHT OUT OF HER HEAD.

YEAH, POOR OLD MISS HAZELNUT DOESN'T STAND A CHANCE.

THAT'S HAZELWOOD, LET'S GET OUT OF HERE BEFORE SOMEONE SEES US.

WHAT ARE YOU GUYS UP TO?

OH HI, JEREMIAH?

OH WE'RE JUST GETTING READY FOR A LITTLE FUN.

TO BE CONTINUED...

THE ADVENTURES OF...

by ©1990
Ron Wheeler
J-20

PANDEMONIUM IS ABOUT TO STRIKE BENTON HIGH FROM MATT AND LUKE'S BOOBY-TRAPPED CLASSROOM

WE'VE GOT TO STOP MISS HAZELWOOD, MATT!

WE CAN'T! THEN SHE'D KNOW WE PLANTED THE BOOBY-TRAPS!

BUT WHAT IF SHE FINDS THE ...

POW!

...EXPLODING PEN.

LOOKS LIKE SHE ALREADY HAS.

EEEK!

WELL THERE'S THE RUBBER SNAKE.

OH YUCK!

NOW SHE FOUND THE FAKE VOMIT. I CAN'T WATCH

THE ADVENTURES OF... JEREMIAH

by ©1990 Roy Wheeler J-21

MATT AND LUKE ARE IN TROUBLE FOR TRYING TO DISRUPT THE SUBSTITUTE TEACHER'S CLASS.

WE'RE SORRY.

YES, MISS HAZELWOOD, WE'VE LEARNED OUR LESSON.

IT WAS WRONG OF US TO BOOBY-TRAP YOUR CLASSROOM WITH RUBBER SNAKES, EXPLODING PENS, FAKE VOMIT, AND WHOOPIE CUSHIONS.

DON'T FORGET THE FROG.

OH YES, THE FROG, TOO.

AND WE SINCERELY DO APOLOGIZE.

AND YES, WE VERY MUCH WOULD LIKE TO STAY AFTER SCHOOL TO TAKE THE HISTORY TEST THAT WAS SCHEDULED.

IT WON'T HAPPEN AGAIN! WE PROMISE! BYE!

WHEW! I'M GLAD THAT'S OVER.

DID YOU GET IT?

THE ADVENTURES OF...

JEREMIAH

by ©1990
RWheeler
J-37

MATT AND LUKE PICK ON THE NEW FOREIGN EXCHANGE STUDENT AT SCHOOL.

HEY, LUKE, WATCH THIS.

SAY, SBLTNK, YOU SHOULDN'T WRITE WITH THAT PEN.

I SHOULDN'T?

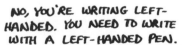

NO, YOU'RE WRITING LEFT-HANDED. YOU NEED TO WRITE WITH A LEFT-HANDED PEN.

I SHOULD?

THAT'S RIGHT. YOU COULD DO SERIOUS DAMAGE TO YOUR METACARPALS.

MY METACARPALS?

THAT'S RIGHT, YOUR METACARPALS ARE THOSE CARP-SHAPED BONES IN YOUR HAND.

THEY ARE?

IF YOU WRITE LEFT-HANDED WITH A RIGHT-HANDED PEN, THE FINS IN YOUR META-CARPALS WILL TURN THE WRONG WAY.

THEY WILL?

TO BE CONTINUED...

TO BE CONTINUED...

THE ADVENTURES OF...

JEREMIAH

by ©1990
Ron Wheeler
J-39

SBLTNK TAKES A LIKING TO MATT.

WHAT'S THE MATTER, MATT?

IT'S THAT SBLTNK!

HE FOLLOWS ME EVERY-WHERE.

I CAN'T GET AWAY FROM HIM.

IT'S AS IF I'M THE ONLY FRIEND HE HAS.

THAT'S PROBABLY BECAUSE YOU ARE.

IT'S NOT EASY FOR MOST AMERICANS TO BEFRIEND FOREIGNERS WHO LOOK AND TALK DIFFERENTLY THAN WE DO.

BUT WHY DOESN'T HE BEFRIEND YOU?

HE DOES AND I AM HIS FRIEND...

...BUT I ALSO KEEP SENDING HIM OVER TO YOU, TOO.

WELL, THANKS A LOT!

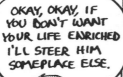

THE ADVENTURES OF...

JEREMIAH

by ©1991
Ron
Wheeler
K-5

MATT STORMS OUT OF THE SCHOOL BUILDING.

BOY! AM I **HOT!**

WHAT'S WRONG, MATT.

LOOK AT THE GRADE I GOT ON MY SCIENCE PAPER.

"C-", HUH? THAT'S NOT TOO GOOD.

I'LL SAY! MY PARENTS ARE GOING TO KILL ME!

WHAT DOES THAT TEACHER HAVE AGAINST ME ANYHOW?

WHAT MAKES YOU THINK IT'S THE TEACHER'S FAULT?

HOW MANY PAGES IS YOUR PAPER?

SEVEN.

SEE? THAT'S THE SAME LENGTH AS MINE.

TO BE CONTINUED...

THE ADVENTURES OF...

JEREMIAH

by ©1991
B. Wheeler
K-7

MATT IS STILL FRUSTRATED ABOUT SCIENCE CLASS.

NOW WHAT?

THE MAN HATES ME.

HE GAVE ME ANOTHER "C-"!

DID YOU DESERVE IT?

OF COURSE NOT. HE HATES ME.

LOOK, JEREMIAH, WOULD YOU PUT IN A GOOD WORD FOR ME? HE LIKES YOU. HE GIVES YOU "A's"!

I STUDY FOR MY "A's". LIKING ME HAS NOTHING TO DO WITH IT.

OH, SURE! SURE!

JUST TALK TO HIM, JEREMIAH.

YOU'VE GOT A STUDENT/TEACHER CONFERENCE WITH HIM THIS AFTERNOON.

TO BE CONTINUED...

THE ADVENTURES OF...

JEREMIAH

by ©1991 Roy Wheeler K-8

JEREMIAH LEARNS SOMETHING IN HIS STUDENT/TEACHER CONFERENCE.

WELL, JEREMIAH, DID YOU TALK TO MR. HOWELL?

YES, I DID.

DID YOU PUT IN A GOOD WORD FOR ME?

NO, HE PUT IN A GOOD WORD FOR YOU!

HUH?

HE SAID YOU HAVE ALL THE MAKINGS OF BEING A GREAT SCIENTIST.

HE DID?

YOU'RE SMART, YOU'RE CREATIVE, YOU'RE ENERGETIC.

I...I AM?

HE SAID ALL THOSE THINGS? REALLY? HE SAID THAT?

BUT HE ALSO SAID THAT YOU ARE USING ALL OF THOSE TRAITS IN THE WRONG DIRECTION!